D1252704

Ponds

Diyan Leake

Heinemann LIBRARY
Chicago, Illinois

© 2015 Heinemann Library
an imprint of Capstone Global Library, LLC
Chicago, Illinois

To contact Capstone Global Library, please call 800-747-4992,
or visit our website www.capstonepub.com

Edited by Joanna Issa and Penny West
Designed by Philippa Jenkins
Original illustrations © Capstone Global Library Ltd 2014
Picture research by Mica Brancic
Production by Helen McCreath
Originated by Capstone Global Library Ltd
Printed and bound in China by Leo Paper Group

18 17 16 15 14
10 9 8 7 6 5 4 3 2 1

Library of Congress Cataloging-in-Publication Data
Leake, Diyan, author.
  Ponds / Diyan Leake.
    pages cm.—(Water, water everywhere!)
  Summary: "In this book, children learn all about ponds,
including what ponds are like, what lives in ponds, how some
ponds are made, and how to stay safe near ponds."—Provided
by publisher.
  Includes bibliographical references and index.
  ISBN 978-1-4846-0452-6 (hb)
  1. Ponds—Juvenile literature. 2. Pond animals—Juvenile
literature. I. Title.

  QH541.5.P63
  551.48'2—dc23   2013039549

Acknowledgments
We would like to thank the following for permission to reproduce
photographs: Alamy pp. 4 (© Arco Images GmbH), 5, 23c
(© Tom Grundy), 8 (© The Photolibrary Wales/Steve Benbow), 10
(© blickwinkel), 11, 22a (© Paul Thompson Images), 16
(© Kelly-marie smith), 17 (© Nicholas Toh), 18 (© Andrew
Horner), 19, 23b (© Cristina Lichti), 20 (© Image Source Plus);
Corbis p. 21 (Blend Images/© Hill Street Studios); FLPA pp.
9 (Minden Pictures/Gerry Ellis), 13 (Malcolm Schuyl); Getty
Images pp. 6, 23a (Stone+/Diane Cook and Len Jenshel);
Shutterstock pp. 7 (© Matt Gibson), 12 (© Wang LiQiang), 14
(© Alexander Potapov), 15 (© Paladin12), 22b (©
WayneImage), 22c (© windu).

Cover photograph reproduced with permission of Shutterstock
(© Tessa Bishop).
Back cover photograph reproduced with permission of
Shutterstock/© Alexander Potapov.

We would like to thank Michael Bright and Nancy Harris for their
invaluable help in the preparation of this book.

Every effort has been made to contact copyright holders of
material reproduced in this book. Any omissions will be rectified
in subsequent printings if notice is given to the publisher.

All the Internet addresses (URLs) given in this book were valid at
the time of going to press. However, due to the dynamic nature
of the Internet, some addresses may have changed, or sites
may have changed or ceased to exist since publication. While
the author and publisher regret any inconvenience this may
cause readers, no responsibility for any such changes can be
accepted by either the author or the publisher.

Contents

Ponds

A pond is a body of water.

A pond has shallow water.

A pond is like a small lake.

A pond has land all around it.

What Makes a Pond?

Some ponds are made by nature.

Beavers made this pond by using tree branches.

Some ponds are made by people.

Some people like to have a
pond in their yard.

Animals in Ponds

Some birds live in ponds.

Some snails live in ponds.

Frogs live in ponds.

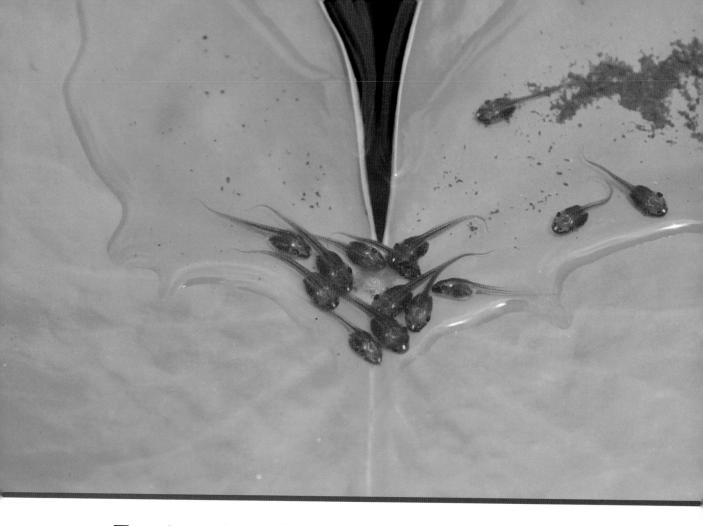

Tadpoles live in ponds.

Some insects live near ponds.

This insect can walk on the water.

Plants in Ponds

Plants live in ponds.

rushes

This duck has made a nest out of rushes.

Having Fun by Ponds

It is fun to spend time by a pond.

Stay safe! Always have an adult with you when you are near water.

Quiz

Which of these is a pond?

A

B

C

Answer on page 24

Picture Glossary

nature everything in the world not made by people or machines

rushes stiff plants that grow in water or on very wet land

shallow not deep

Index

Answer to quiz on page 22: Picture **A** shows a pond.

Note to Parents and Teachers
Before reading
Show the children the photograph on the cover of the book. Can they say what kind of water the photograph shows? Can they name some of the animals that might live there? Have they ever seen a pond? What did they do while they were there? Do any of the children have a pond in their yard?

After reading
- Plan a pond visit with the children. Before you go on your trip, ask them to draw the animals and plants they would expect to see in or around the pond. Show them pictures of animals and plants that are common in your area.
- Show the children the picture of tadpoles on page 15 again. Ask them if they know what animal a tadpole grows into. Use cutouts of the different life stages of a frog to talk about how a tadpole changes.